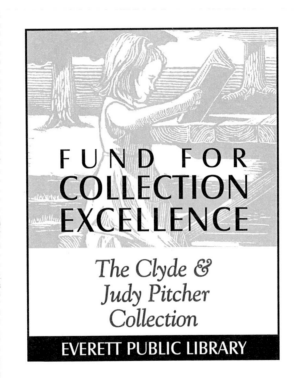

SPENDING SPREE

THE HISTORY OF AMERICAN SHOPPING

CYNTHIA OVERBECK BIX

TFCB

TWENTY-FIRST CENTURY BOOKS / MINNEAPOLIS

To my family—especially my dear mother and sister, my first and best shopping companions. Special thanks to my editor, Domenica Di Piazza, for her unerring guidance and skill in bringing this book to life

Twenty-First Century Books
A division of Lerner Publishing Group, Inc.
241 First Avenue North
Minneapolis, MN 55401 U.S.A.

Website address: www.lernerbooks.com

Library of Congress Cataloging-in-Publication Data

Bix, Cynthia Overbeck.
    Spending spree : the history of American shopping / by Cynthia Overbeck Bix.
       pages   cm
    Includes bibliographical references and index.
    ISBN 978–1–4677–1017–6 (lib. bdg. : alk. paper)
    ISBN 978–1–4677–1658–1 (eBook)
    1. Retail trade—United States—History. 2. Stores, Retail—United States—History. 3. Shopping malls—United States—History. 4. Consumers—United States—History. I. Title.
    HF5429.3.B59 2014
    381'.10973—dc23   2012050486

Manufactured in the United States of America
1 – BP – 7/15/13

CONTENTS

CHAPTER 1
A NATION DISCOVERS SHOPPING

Chewers [of tobacco] will please spit at each other and not on the floor. Only one free match to a customer.

–Larry Freeman, *The Country Store*, signs in a general store, early 1800s

Want to go shopping? You probably either head for the mall with your friends or touch the screen of your smartphone or iPad to get to your favorite online shopping sites. But two hundred years ago? No way. Shopping usually meant a long trip in a horse-drawn wagon with your parents to a cramped, dimly lit wooden shop on the main road of the nearest tiny town. A shopkeeper in his white apron would be standing behind a long wooden counter. Your mom might point to a bolt of cotton fabric on the shelf behind him and ask to see it. The shopkeeper would be the one to measure out a length. Meanwhile, your dad would be cracking jokes with a group of fellow farmers by the shop's wood-burning stove. They would probably be talking about crops, so the shopkeeper would show them handsaws and other shiny, new tools. You and your siblings would be looking longingly—not at tablets or skinny jeans—but at a display of pretty hair ribbons and at a glass jar full of peppermints on the counter.

This is exactly the scene at Gray's General Store in Adamsville, Rhode Island, in July 1800. Gray's has been in business for twelve years, and it's the one-and-only place for most local people to buy everything from material for sewing clothes, to flour for bread

General stores such as Gray's *(above)* in Rhode Island served the retail needs of surrounding communities for more than two hundred years. When it closed in 2012, it was the oldest continuously operating general store in the United States.

making, to teakettles and brooms. (Gray's operated for another one hundred years before finally closing its doors in 2012.)

In the twenty-first century, stores of all sizes and kinds are everywhere. They line the streets of cities and towns. They crowd shopping malls and dot the edges of highways. You can even do some great shopping in airports and at museum gift shops. Televisions and computers offer instantaneous twenty-four-hour shopping. Everywhere there's a dizzying array of products. Multiple brands of smartphones, jeans, shoes, backpacks, breakfast cereals, microwaves, televisions, computers, bedding, dishes, vacuum cleaners, pet products, and more crowd shelves.

People shop to get groceries, toothpaste, and all the other things they really need for everyday living. But they also shop for things they want. Like the latest skateboard or that fun strapless summer dress. Buying these nonessentials gives people's spirits a lift and makes them feel as though they are keeping up with the trends. Shopping is recreation too—an outing to the mall, a vacation pleasure, or something to do with friends on a Saturday afternoon.

In the nation's early years, however, things were very different. Few goods were available to buy. Ordinary people made most of what they needed—and wanted—themselves. They shopped only for manufactured basics they couldn't make on their own.

What happened to change all this? How did the United States become the world's biggest consumer market? The answer lies in the growth of the nation itself—in the shift from farms to cities and then to the suburbs, and in the rise of the American middle class, with newfound leisure time and money to spend.

COUNTRY WAYS

In early America, Native Americans across the continent used a system of barter, exchanging goods or services without using money. They traded things they considered of equal value, such as an animal hide for a handcrafted item such as a basket, or meat for corn. A lot of trading took place among different tribes, who traveled over established trade routes. Once Europeans arrived, Native Americans also traded with them, exchanging food, furs,

In colonial America, bartering was common. For example, Native Americans in woodland areas of North America provided prized beaver pelts to Europeans in exchange for manufactured goods such as pots and pans.

and animal hides for metal knives and pots, woven cloth, and other manufactured goods.

Until the early 1800s, most non-native people in the United States lived in the countryside, on farms and in little towns. Just a few cities, such as New York, Boston, and Philadelphia, were large population centers where culture and large-scale commerce took place.

People in the countryside grew their own vegetables and raised livestock for milk and meat. They made most things they owned by hand. A person had just one or two pieces of clothing for everyday wear. Rural houses were equipped with a few pieces of simple hand-hewn furniture. Children worked alongside their parents as soon as they were able and had little time for toys and games. A girl might have one rag doll sewed by her ma. A boy might have a wooden top carved by his pa.

In the 1800s, growing, harvesting, and preparing food was hard work for people who did not live in cities with easy access to stores. In this image from the 1890s, a farm family poses in their wheat field with a horse-drawn, mechanical reaper.

Almost all manufactured goods were shipped into the United States from Britain. Yet imported things were expensive. They were mostly available only in big cities, where wealthy citizens could afford them. Most ordinary Americans could count their manufactured possessions on the fingers of two hands. Many of these were precious family heirlooms.

DOOR-TO-DOOR

Manufactured goods that did make their way into the countryside came in the trunks and horse-drawn wagons of roving peddlers. Peddlers brought American commerce into the countryside and began to create a larger consumer market for goods. One young

Peddlers sold a range of goods in the countryside. This peddler, in an image dated 1889, presented his goods to buyers in Littleton, New Hampshire.

man named James Guild, who roamed the back roads of New England in the 1820s, took a trunk of merchandise and set out west from his farm home in Vermont. At each country house, he knocked on the door and asked, "Do you wish to buy some hare [hair] combs, needles, buttons, button molds, sewing silk, beads?"

Early peddlers were the forerunners of traveling salesmen. After the American Civil War (1861–1865), these salesmen spread out across the country. They worked for the new and rising New York and Philadelphia wholesalers, who bought merchandise in large amounts from manufacturers and resold it to consumers. The salesmen sold hardware, medicines, shoes, and dry goods such as fabric for sewing, hats, and accessories. Traveling salesmen became familiar figures from the 1860s up until the 1920s. They were known as drummers because they "beat the drum," or "drummed up business" for their merchandise. Like peddlers, they went door-to-door or called on small local stores. They sold products such as Uneeda Biscuit, Ivory soap, Kingsford's laundry starch, and Clabber Girl Baking Powder. Some salesmen set up shop in a public place and hawked their wares from a wagon. They were flashy dressers who brought an air of big-city sophistication to country folk. Author Don Marquis describes being spellbound by one of these salesmen as a boy. "My memory still retains a picture of myself, as a barefooted, freckle-faced boy of twelve, standing on a plank sidewalk in a prairie town . . . and looking up at one of these magnificent beings."

Many salesmen were honest and believed in their products. But others were out to swindle customers. Some sold useless patent medicines to unsuspecting country folks. One medicine, Dr. Flint's Quaker Bitters (made mostly of alcohol), claimed to cure nervousness, stomach problems, pimples, headaches, dizziness, and more.

CRACKER-BARREL COMMERCE

In many rural communities, people bought goods in country stores. Also called general stores, these were central gathering places for people who lived isolated lives far from other families. A general store was usually the only store in town. Most general stores were small, cramped one-story buildings filled with a hodgepodge of merchandise. Tin cans of baking powder, tea, and other groceries lined shelves behind the counter. Tall wooden butter churns, brooms, and chamber pots sat on the floor. Hanging from ceiling hooks were kerosene lanterns and pots and pans. Many foods were sold in bulk rather than in packages. Big wooden barrels held foods such as crackers and pickles. On the counter was a large scale for weighing flour, salt, and other bulk items.

General stores provided goods as well as social outlets to families across the country. As in this photo of a general store in Oklahoma in the late 1800s, entire families shopped together. Parents caught up on local news while they chose tools, food, and fabric. Kids might get a piece of penny candy.

Shopping was a personal, face-to-face experience. The shopkeeper knew all his customers by name. In an age before telephones, the farmer's wife might see her neighbors at the shop and catch up on the latest gossip. The farmer could chew tobacco *and* "chew the fat" (gossip) with other men. The shopkeeper was usually a trusted member of the community. He always knew the going price of wheat or the latest happenings in the nearest city, where he went twice a year to purchase the goods he sold.

At this time in U.S. history, shopping was not recreation. Customers couldn't browse up and down aisles of merchandise and pick out what they wanted. Most things were behind the sales counter. The customer had to ask the shopkeeper to pull down a teapot from the shelf or to measure out a pound of flour onto a piece of paper and wrap it up. (Paper bags weren't in use until after the Civil War, and plastic wasn't common until the 1960s.)

Prices weren't marked. Instead, the shopkeeper and the customer bargained to agree on a price. Payment was either in cash or on store credit, which the store owner tracked through notes in his ledger book. Sometimes people could barter, exchanging produce from their farms for merchandise.

In the late 1800s, manufacturers of flour, laundry starch, crackers, and other items began to put their products in small packages instead of selling them to shopkeepers in bulk. They also set uniform prices. For example, the National Biscuit Company (later Nabisco) sold five-cent packages of soda crackers labeled with the catchy name "Uneeda Biscuit." A pound of Chase & Sanborn coffee came packed in a colorful can. People especially liked the new packaged food products, which seemed more sanitary than foods the shopkeeper pulled out of open barrels.

READY, SET, SHOP!

After the Civil War, railroads expanded all over the country. They provided fast, ready connections to the larger world. Before the

Trains were often a happy sight in nineteenth-century America. Passenger trains such as this one carried friends and family across long distances, while freight trains brought a wide range of manufactured goods to market in record time.

railroads, men moved imported goods from the port cities of New York and Boston to the rest of the country using horse- or ox-drawn wagons or river and canal boats. In 1830 such a trip took three weeks from New York to Chicago. But by 1880, trains made it possible for the same goods to make the same journey in less than twenty-four hours. Every town wanted to be on a railroad line. Whole towns even moved, relocating closer to a new line.

By the late 1800s, new factories were springing up in the United States. Powered by newly invented steam engines and staffed by hundreds of workers, the factories manufactured goods much faster than was possible by hand. Cloth mills in Lowell, Massachusetts, churned out thousands of yards of cotton fabric. Hat factories in Danbury, Connecticut, produced hundreds and hundreds of men's hats. The Waterbury Button Company in Connecticut supplied metal, cloth, and ivory buttons.

Advances in American manufacturing meant that fewer goods had to come from overseas. This led to lower prices, which in turn meant that more people could afford them. As manufactured goods became available, more shops opened to sell them. Goods were still mostly available in cities, but soon they became available in small towns too.

MAIL-ORDER MADNESS

For many country people, mail-order catalogs were a lifesaver. In fact, mail-order catalogs were often called the Farmer's Bible. In the twenty-first century, it's hard to imagine how isolated Americans once were. Mail-order catalogs were a link to the outside world as well as a source for manufactured goods. The postal service charged companies very little to mail the catalogs, and railroads brought the goods people ordered to rural areas and small towns. Popular American entertainment reflected some of the excitement. For example, in the song "Wells Fargo Wagon" from a popular 1957 Broadway musical called *The Music Man,*

the citizens of River City, Iowa, anticipate the arrival of a mail-order rocking chair, some maple sugar, new curtains, and a crosscut saw.

One of the first U.S. mail-order companies was Montgomery Ward, which started in 1872. Sears, Roebuck and Company followed in 1886. Founder Richard Sears called his 1894 catalog the "Book of Bargains: A Money Saver for Everyone." In it, he offered almost every kind of merchandise imaginable—

Mail-order catalogs, such as this Sears, Roebuck and Company catalog from 1899, offered a dazzling array of goods. The voluminous catalogs, while practical, offered insight into the latest styles and innovations in an era of rapid manufacturing growth.

saddles, sewing machines, baby carriages, shoes, blouses, musical instruments, buggies, books, and even the new Edison Gramophone Talking Machine. Black-and-white drawings showed what the products looked like.

Americans spent hours poring over the catalogs. Montgomery Ward's catalog of the 1890s, called the Great Wish Book, was 544 pages long and offered twenty-four thousand items. Sears topped it in 1897 with a 786-page catalog. Later, the Sears catalog offered actual houses for sale. Its Modern Homes program sold blueprints for 447 different styles of homes. Precut and numbered lumber, doors, windows, and roofing were shipped by rail to the buyer for assembly. For some styles, an outhouse (outdoor toilet) could be bought separately. The company sold more than 75,000 of these homes between 1908 and 1940. Many still stand in neighborhoods all over the United States.

Mail order is still big business. Catalogs from Tilly's, Alloy, Urban Outfitters, and other manufacturers fill mailboxes—and are available online. Many people buy through mail order not because they can't get out to shop but because it's quick and easy to shop the catalog way.

THE NEW CONSUMERS

The rise of American manufacturing in the late 1800s also created a new middle class, people with jobs who had a little extra money at the end of each month for luxury purchases. In addition, more people—especially women—had newfound leisure time.

As the U.S. economy developed in the 1800s, more Americans had money to spend on nonessentials. With more leisure time, they could shop for beautiful luxury items such as this Wedgewood coffee cup and saucer imported from England.

They could use their free time to shop. No longer satisfied with just the bare necessities, shoppers wanted the latest styles in shoes and hats from New York, elegant glassware and china, or a shiny new brass bed. As French historian and observer of U.S. culture Alexis de Tocqueville observed, Americans were beginning to take "pleasures in material life."

Then, as now, many people measured their social status and success by the number and quality of things they owned. In his groundbreaking book, *The Theory of the Leisure Class,* published in 1899, sociologist and economist Thorstein Veblen coined the term *conspicuous consumption*. By this he meant the spending of money for things that were not essential to living, to show off one's economic success and high social standing. He identified the new leisure class as those who didn't have to spend all their time working and earning money.

Some observers criticized the new consumerism. Early sociologists pointed out that people had once taken their moral

BETSY AND TACY GO SHOPPING

In her beloved Betsy-Tacy children's books, Maude Hart Lovelace describes the fictional small town of Deep Valley, Minnesota, at the end of the 1800s. In *Betsy and Tacy Go Downtown,* Betsy and her friends shop downtown at Christmastime, on a pretend buying spree. "At the Lion Department Store [a small local store] . . . they chose rhinestone side combs, jeweled hat pins, . . . fluffy collars and belts and pocket books. . . . They went to the drug store where they . . . sniffed every kind of perfume in the store. . . . At the toy shop . . . they inspected doll dishes, doll stoves, sets of shiny doll tinware, doll parlor sets."

values from religion and their happiness from working hard and doing good. Americans were instead getting satisfaction through material goods, a trend that worried some people.

STROLLING DOWN MAIN STREET

Towns gradually grew from a little string of scattered buildings along a dirt road to a main street lined with stores and businesses such as banks, barbershops, and hotels. Instead of one general store where customers bought everything, small mom-and-pop stores on Main Street specialized in different kinds of merchandise. Shoppers could choose from a hardware store, dress shop, grocery store, furniture store, and a small local department store. The local drugstore often had a soda fountain with tall stools along a counter. People could stop in for a cold soda or a dish of ice cream. Because the shops were locally owned, each had its own character and style. A ladies' dress shop in Greenville, Ohio, would be different in character from one in Abingdon, Virginia, and it would have a different selection of clothes to buy.

As in earlier general stores, shopping on small-town Main Street was face-to-face and personal. The shopkeepers and salesclerks were local people. Everyone knew one another. Customers relied on the guidance of shop clerks in selecting the best armchair or the latest spring dress or the right size wood screws.

DISNEY DOES MAIN STREET

The Disneyland attraction "Main Street, U.S.A." in Anaheim, California, is an idealized re-creation of an 1890s small-town street. A Disneyland brochure greets visitors with, "Welcome, neighbor! Wherever you come from, this is your hometown. The kind of place you stroll through, stopping to visit your favorite shop, . . . [and] listen to the sweet harmony of a barbershop quartet."

CHAPTER 2

SHOPPING GOES BIG TIME

All America goes to New York for its shopping when it can.

—Moses King, *King's Handbook of New York City*, 1892

Broadway runs the length of the island of Manhattan in New York City. It was *the* place to shop in early 1900s America. This photo from 1890 shows the view north from Murray Street.

In the 1800s, New York City was the nation's commercial leader. On Broadway—the city's main thoroughfare—scores of small stores attracted a steady flow of people. Horse-drawn wagons, carriages, and streetcars jostled in the streets.

In *Sister Carrie,* a classic American novel by Theodore Dreiser from 1900, the main character, Carrie, walks down Broadway in New York. "Jewelers' windows gleamed along the path with remarkable frequency. Florist shops, furriers, haberdashers [dealers in men's clothes], confectioners, all followed in rapid procession. The street was full of coaches. Pompous doormen, in immense coats with shiny brass belts and buttons, waited in front of expensive salesrooms. Coachmen . . . waited . . . for the mistresses of carriages, who were shopping inside. The whole street bore the flavor of riches and show."

A NEW KIND OF SHOPPING

In 1848 an exciting new kind of store opened on Broadway. A merchant named A. T. Stewart built the spectacular Marble Palace. This four-story marble-fronted building was unlike any other store. In fact, it was more like a museum. Stewart's store was a marvel with its grand staircases, high ceilings, central rotunda, and hundreds of windows.

Stewart sold fancy women's clothing and accessories. The store also introduced a brand-new idea—organizing merchandise by departments. It had a ribbon department and a hat department. Shoppers could also browse in departments for silks, woolens, and other fabrics. Clerks would "cut off a dress," meaning they would cut enough fabric for the customer to make a dress (or have one made for her). Although ready-made clothes for women had not yet become widely available, Stewart's did offer some ready-made garments such as corsets, capes, and furs. They even sold shawls for a whopping $1,000. Women could try on clothing in the Ladies' Parlor in front of full-length mirrors from Paris, which were an innovation at the time.

Soon other merchants caught on to the department store idea. Like Stewart's, most of them were focused on selling dry goods. Many—R. H. Macy & Company, B. Altman, and Lord & Taylor—were built on a stretch of Broadway and Sixth Avenue, between 9th Street and 23rd Street. During the 1870s, this area became known as Ladies' Mile. By all accounts, Ladies' Mile was a sparkling, exciting place. *King's Handbook of New York City,* published in 1892, extolled the "fascinating, alluring, irresistible" shops.

Everyone came to Ladies' Mile to admire and shop. One of the most famous customers on Ladies' Mile was Mary Todd Lincoln, wife of President Abraham Lincoln. She shopped constantly and was criticized by the press for spending money beyond her means. At one time, she was reported to have bought one hundred pairs of gloves in one four-month period!

BEYOND NEW YORK

Not all newfangled department stores were in New York City. Department stores sprang up in cities all over the United States. By about 1900, just about every American city had its own large department store in the heart of downtown.

R. H. Macy was one of the nation's first department stores. This photo of the store in New York City dates to the early 1930s.

One of the earliest was Wanamaker's, founded in 1876 in Philadelphia, Pennsylvania. This "New Kind of Store" covered 3 acres. In addition to merchandise sold at 129 counters, Wanamaker's had a restaurant and offered U.S parcel post delivery. Eventually, the store even sold cars. Other groundbreaking department stores included the Emporium in San Francisco, California; Dayton's Department Store in Minneapolis, Minnesota; and the elegant Maison Blanche in New Orleans, Louisiana. In Boston the Jordan Marsh department store offered fashion shows, a bakery famous for its blueberry muffins, art exhibitions, and even afternoon concerts.

Chicago's great department store, Marshall Field & Company, began in 1862 as a modest dry goods store. Started by Potter Palmer, Field's was a high-class establishment. After growing and moving several times, the Marshall Field's store on State Street "was dominated by quiet elegance, starting at its entrance, with doormen . . . who brushed snow off coats and checked parcels and umbrellas, to wood-panelled libraries and waiting rooms with maids for service."

"Give the lady what she wants."

—Marshall Field, department store founder, slogan, 1800s

"SPLENDOR AND BEAUTY"

The department store buildings themselves drew people in and made them want to shop. One observer called the stores a "fairyland" and a scene of "splendor and of beauty." They rose many stories high and sometimes took up entire city blocks. When customers walked in, they stepped onto elegant marble floors. Wide aisles defined by big columns and high ceilings gave an impression of light and space. Sometimes a high central rotunda, with plenty of glass, added grandeur and more light. In Chicago's Marshall Field's 1907 store, the central grand dome was designed by glass artist Louis Comfort Tiffany. It was made up of 1.6 million pieces of handblown iridescent glass.

To move customers to the upper floors, department stores installed elevators as early as the 1860s. The first elevators were powered by huge steam boilers in the basement. The steam powered ropes or cables that wound around a drum and lifted the cars. Later models were hydraulic. Water pressure pushed them upward and slowly drained as they went down. Instead of push buttons to operate the elevators, white-gloved

Elevators were new in the mid-1800s. Elevator operators, such as this woman in 1930s Cincinnati, Ohio, greeted department store shoppers and manually operated the lifts from floor to floor.

Salesclerks in department stores offered individual attention and personalized service to shoppers. This photo, dated 1916, shows shoppers in a women's wear department.

elevator operators, both male and female, manually opened the doors for customers to go in and out. Wooden escalators, called moving stairways, provided another way to move people to the upper floors. Bloomingdale's in New York claimed to have the first escalators, installed in 1898.

Early department stores were lit by gaslights. But these lamps were dim and flickering, and it was hard to see merchandise in the gloom. When electric light came on in New York in 1882, the stores eagerly took it up. Electroliers—electric chandeliers—lit up department stores inside and out.

Department stores tended to be divided into two main classes. High-class stores, such as Stewart's and B. Altman in New York, catered to wealthy and stylish clientele. These well-heeled customers were sometimes known as the carriage trade because they could afford fancy carriages to take them shopping. As in earlier eras, customers could buy on store credit instead of paying

While upper- and middle-class shoppers enjoyed themselves in the big stores on Broadway and Ladies' Mile, the scene was very different on the Lower East Side and in other poor neighborhoods of New York. There, recent immigrants and other low-income residents of the city did most of their shopping at outdoor markets along the streets.

From stands on the sidewalk, vendors sold everything from produce, meat, and fish to newspapers and cigars. New York journalist James D. McCabe Jr. reported in the 1870s that "watches, jewelry . . . fruits, tobacco . . . candies, cakes, ice cream, lemonade, flowers, dogs, birds—in short, everything that can be carried in the hand—are sold by the Street Vendors."

A familiar figure was the pushcart man. These men pushed small, wheeled carts along the streets. Many sold fruits and vegetables, as well as prepared foods such as hot potatoes, pickles, or pretzels. Although their beginnings were humble, some pushcart businesses eventually grew to be brick-and-mortar stores. ABC Carpet & Home in New York (and online) started out in 1897 as a pushcart business selling floor coverings. The famous New York delicatessen-style store, Russ & Daughters, began around 1900 as Joel Russ's Polish mushroom pushcart.

cash. Salesclerks showered personal attention on customers, getting merchandise from drawers and cabinets behind the counters and wrapping up purchases with special care.

On the other hand, bargain stores served working people and thrifty middle-income shoppers. Many of these consumers were workers—male and female—who were pouring into the cities to work in the new factories and offices. The stores sold merchandise at low prices. They ordered goods in bulk and heaped them onto tables in a jumble that suggested there were great bargains to be found.

Some of the bargain stores were unattractive, with harsh lights and scuffed floors. But Macy's and others—such as New York's Siegel-Cooper store, which opened in 1896—aimed to attract middle-class shoppers by providing attractive decor and polite service for everyone.

On the Lower East Side of New York City in 1895, residents bought vegetables from stands on the street.

FOR THE LADIES AND GENTS

During the golden age of department stores (roughly from the 1880s through the 1920s), department stores aimed most of their attractions at women. Retailers quickly saw that women did the most shopping, especially for clothes. When women's ready-to-wear clothing became widely available around 1915, department stores began to sell ready-made clothes instead of only fabric. In addition, the stores carried jewelry, perfume, handbags, and other women's accessories and luxuries.

To make women feel comfortable in an age when it wasn't proper for them to go out alone, stores offered many new kinds of services. They added restrooms equipped with a lounge where women could sit and rest as well as use toilet facilities.

Tearooms and lunchrooms in the stores offered places to have a leisurely meal. These were often elegant, with big windows and chandeliers. They served everything from soups and sandwiches to hot, full-course meals. The eighth floor of the 1902 Macy's store in

Shoppers at Marshall Field's in Chicago, Illinois, enjoy a leisurely meal in the store's elegant tearoom. In the early 1900s (the era of this photo), women often spent the whole day in a single store.

New York's Herald Square was the site of a restaurant so big it could seat twenty-five hundred people. Later, some tearooms entertained diners with small orchestras as well as live fashion shows. With access to toilets, lunchrooms, and entertainment, women could comfortably spend hours—or even a whole day—in a single store.

"Wearing hats and gloves to shop and eating sandwiches in the tearoom while models paraded by, and requesting certain tunes to be played on the store organ, are as foreign to a young shopper at Wal-Mart as living in a Venetian palace."

—Ann Satterthwaite, *Going Shopping,* 2001

Before department stores, men could buy clothing at specialty shops. The Gentlemen's Fashionable Wearing Apparel Warehouse opened in New York in 1816. Brooks Clothing Store (later Brooks Brothers), opened there two years later. Along with custom-made and ready-made coats, jackets, and trousers, these stores sold accessories such as suspenders, socks, cravats (neckties), and handkerchiefs.

The new department stores wanted to attract male shoppers. They began to offer high-quality men's ready-made clothes, as well as cigars, liquor, and other men's items. Eventually the stores added entire floors devoted just to men's furnishings. They also put in wood-paneled grill restaurants and smoking rooms for men only.

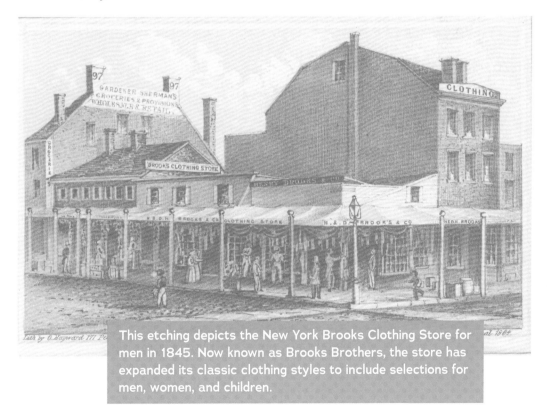

This etching depicts the New York Brooks Clothing Store for men in 1845. Now known as Brooks Brothers, the store has expanded its classic clothing styles to include selections for men, women, and children.

DEPARTMENTS GALORE

As time went on, department stores offered more merchandise beyond clothing. At first, they added household items such as china and glassware. Gradually, the selection expanded, so that large stores such as Macy's might have as many as 150 departments, each specializing in different categories of goods. Soon, shoppers could buy everything from dresses and socks to cribs and armchairs.

The departments were arranged in ways designed to lure customers in from the street and then encourage them to explore the store's upper floors. Retailers reserved the ground floor for frivolous, fun items such as candy, jewelry, cosmetics, perfume, and women's shoes, which shoppers were more likely to buy on impulse. Sometimes men's clothing and shoes were on the first floor too. The upper floors were for necessities, such as underwear or rugs, that people would search out in the store even if they weren't the first things they saw. Theodore Dreiser's heroine, Carrie, "passed along the busy aisles, much affected by the remarkable displays of trinkets, dress goods, shoes, stationery, jewelry. Each separate counter was a show place of dazzling interest and attraction."

The next floors usually held—in ascending order—women's clothing and lingerie; children's clothing and toys; china and glassware; housewares and linens; books and stationery items; and, at the very top floor, furniture and rugs. Even on the upper floors, though, some departments were elaborately decorated. In the 1930s, a department store in Saint Louis, Missouri, decorated its evening gown department to look like a glamorous nightclub. In its book department, Marshall Field's displayed books in a setting that copied the sidewalk bookstalls along the Seine River in Paris. Toy departments were magical realms for children—wonderlands of pedal cars, electric trains, kites, dolls, and dollhouses.

WINDOW SHOPPING

From the early days of department stores, display windows were major attractions on city streets. Large plate glass windows held lavish, colorful displays that were designed to catch the eyes of passersby and lure them inside to shop.

In the 1890s, most window decorators were men. L. Frank Baum, author of *The Wonderful Wizard of Oz,* actually earned his living as a window decorator in Chicago. He founded the National Association of Window Trimmers. Gradually, women became window decorators too. As time went on, window displays in higher-class stores became more and more inventive. Moving mechanical figures drew crowds. L. Frank Baum explained that

Christmas window displays have enchanted children and adults for more than one hundred years. In this photo from 1910, passersby admire toys in a Santa and reindeer display.

"people . . . will always stop to examine any thing that moves, and will enjoy. . . wondering how the effect has been maintained." Animated dolls, circus animals, and other delights were sure crowd-pleasers. In an age without television or computers, these large, bright store windows were exciting.

Electric lights allowed window designers to add another dimension of excitement. Author William Leach reports, "A different color 'dramatized' every window at Gimbel's [in New York] . . . purple light on silverware, green on silk, blue on furniture and red on a bedroom inspired by Japanese designs." In 1939 avant-garde artist Salvador Dalí designed windows for New York's Bonwit Teller featuring a mannequin sleeping on a bed of coals, and a fur-lined bathtub. The display outraged so many people that the store changed it. When Dalí saw the changes, he got into the window and overturned the bathtub, which crashed through the plate glass onto the street!

The most beloved store window extravaganzas for many people were—and still are—Christmas holiday displays. The Christmas window tradition started with New York's R. H. Macy & Company in the 1880s. Their large windows displayed a magical fairyland parade of kings, queens, swans, and circus figures, led by Santa in a sleigh pulled by a life-sized reindeer. Soon almost every large store had a spectacular display. It became a tradition in many families to take a special holiday trip downtown to see the windows. Children and adults alike gazed at animated fantasy scenes, electric train displays, and even live animals.

THE OTHER SIDE OF THE COUNTER

Department stores offered employment to a variety of people. The youngest workers were the cash boys. When a customer was ready to pay for an item, the clerk called out, "Cash!" or "Here, boy!" A cash boy took the sales check and the money to a central cashier. The cashier made change, and the boy ran back with it. The boys were grade-school age, and the work was exhausting. When social reformers began to call out the boys' hard work, stores developed a system of small rails or wires by which cash could be sent back and forth in little boxes.

Around 1900 a newer system was used. At Macy's, 18 miles of brass tubes used the power of compressed air to send money from the sales counters to cashiers. The salesclerk put the sales check and the cash into a capsule container and inserted it into the tube. Air pressure sent the capsule down to the basement, where rows of women sat, ready to make change and send it back up in the tubes.

Eventually, most stores decentralized the cashiers and installed cash registers in every department. The cash register first appeared in 1879, invented by a saloonkeeper named James Ritty. Until then, stores had collected money from customers and simply put it in a drawer. But they had no accurate way to keep track of transactions. Ritty's Incorruptible Cashier had metal keys labeled

A replica of James Ritty's original cash register was placed in the Smithsonian Institution in Washington, DC, in 1959.

with monetary denominations. The cash register operator tapped the keys, the cash drawer opened, and a bell rang. The machine also had a built-in adding device that could keep track of a whole day's transactions.

Both men and women worked as salesclerks and operated the cash registers at the department store counters. All clerks worked long hours and sometimes had to be on their feet for ten hours a day, with only a forty-five-minute dinner break. Some protested and won the right to sit on stools when they weren't busy. However, women clerks were paid less than the men, and few women had opportunities for advancement.

Some women did rise to greater heights. In 1862 eighteen-year-old Margaret S. Getchell applied for a job at Macy's. When Rowland Macy interviewed her, he was impressed by her intelligence and confidence. He made her a cashier. Getchell came up with all sorts of ideas for new merchandise, such as soaps, hats, and various types of ready-made ladies' capes and infant wear. She arranged creative merchandise displays and introduced the idea of the store staying open late on Christmas Eve to accommodate last-minute shoppers. In 1866 Getchell was named store superintendent. She was the first woman in the retail world to hold such a position.

EXPANSION AND PUSHBACK

Because of the volume of their sales, department stores could afford to order merchandise in large quantities. So they often sold goods at lower prices than smaller specialty stores. Large bargain department stores offered low prices. Other department stores often held sales and promoted special markdowns on merchandise.

Many owners of small shops felt threatened by the large stores' power. They complained that the stores took away their business, which was often true. They also claimed that "it is the aggregation [large selection] of stock [goods] and prices which attract the customers, and not the quality and selection of goods displayed." Small-store owners considered themselves experts on their particular line of merchandise, such as books, jewelry, or linens. They pointed out that department store clerks often didn't know much about what they were selling.

However, department stores remained popular with shoppers. They weathered the economic ups and downs of the next twenty-five years, through World War I (1914–1918), the Great Depression (1929–1942), and World War II (1939–1945). Through the 1950s and the 1960s, department stores continued to be most people's go-to place for shopping. In the days before women joined the workforce in large numbers, a day of shopping was a popular form of social outing, either with friends or with their children. But by the 1970s, old-style department stores were facing stiff competition from chain stores, discount stores, and big-box stores. Many finally closed in the 1990s.

After the 1995 closing of Washington, DC's beloved 115-year-old Woodward & Lothrop store, Roxanne Roberts wrote in the *Washington Post*, "Farewell to the days of the downtown department store . . . where ladies put on hats and gloves to shop for sheets."

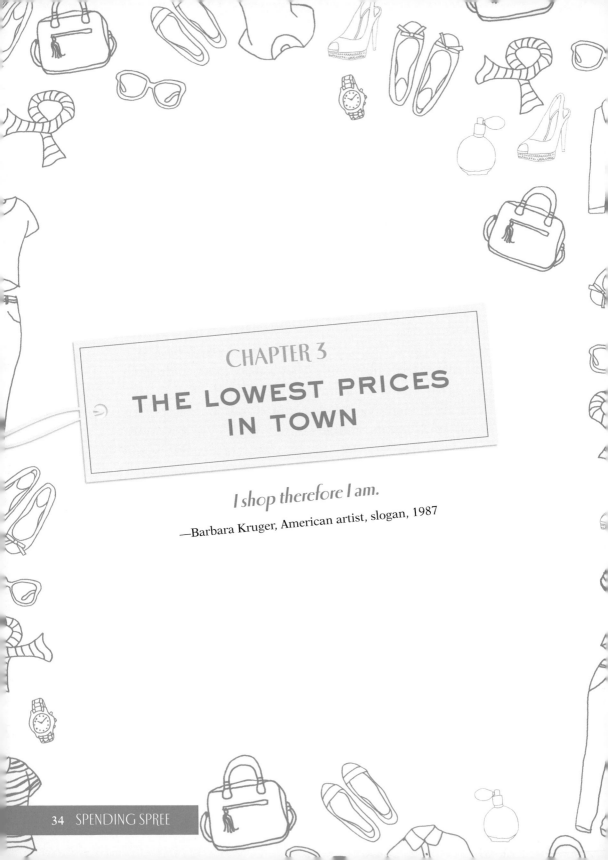

CHAPTER 3

THE LOWEST PRICES IN TOWN

I shop therefore I am.

—Barbara Kruger, American artist, slogan, 1987

Americans love a bargain. Low prices have always been a draw for shoppers—even those with plenty of money. As early as 1827, Frances Trollope, a British visitor to the United States, observed, "I was amused by a national trait which met me at [a store in New York]. I entered it to purchase some *eau de Cologne*, but finding what was offered to me extremely bad, and very cheap, I asked if they had none at a higher price, and better. 'You are a stranger, I guess,' was the answer. 'The Yankees want low price, that's all; they don't [care] so much for goodness as the English.'"

LINKS IN A CHAIN

The introduction of chain stores in the early 1900s made huge changes in the way people shopped. Chain stores are individual stores that are all owned by a central company. Each store in the chain deals in the same merchandise as all the others. This makes it possible for the company to buy merchandise cheaply and in huge quantities so that prices to the customer are relatively low. Chain stores competed with mom-and-pop stores in small towns and eventually put most of them out of business. They even threatened department store sales.

The first chain in the United States was a grocery store. In 1859 the Great Atlantic and Pacific Tea Company began selling tea and coffee in New York. By the early 1900s, under its shortened name, A&P, it had added other grocery items. With the railroad available to ship goods all over the country, A&P had ten thousand stores by 1923.

Similar grocery stores such as Piggly Wiggly followed A&P's example. The Piggly Wiggly chain introduced a new idea: self-service. Instead of receiving personal attention from salesclerks, customers picked out what they wanted from open shelves. Most everything was prepackaged. With self-service, the role of salesclerks changed from personalized service to managing

Famed American photographer Berenice Abbott took this photo of an A&P store in New York City in 1936. The grocery was the first chain store in the United States.

checkout. In most stores, checkout workers punched in sales at the cash register or the supermarket checkout counter. And because self-service meant that stores needed fewer employees, chains could save money on staff, passing along the savings to customers through lower prices.

SHOPPING AT THE FIVE-AND-DIME

One of the earliest and most successful non-grocery chain stores was F. W. Woolworth Company. Its first store, which opened in Pennsylvania in 1879, was called Woolworth's Great Five Cent Store. It had a policy of selling nothing that cost more than a nickel. People flocked to Woolworth's. By 1919 Woolworth's had 1,081 stores in several states. Eventually Woolworth's stores could be found across the entire nation. In 1913 the company built grand headquarters—the Woolworth Building in New York City. It was one of the earliest skyscrapers, and until 1930, it was the world's tallest building.

Woolworth's led the way in the development of the classic American five-and-dime. This photo of the New York City store dates to the mid-1930s.

> *"We bought our make-up at Liggett's Drug Store on the corner of 65th and Madison [in New York City]. We'd sit at the counter and order grilled-cheese sandwiches and cherry cokes while we talked about what color nail polish to buy."*
>
> —Ilene Beckerman, *Love, Loss, and What I Wore*, a 1995 memoir set in New York in the 1950s

Other five-and-dime stores, also called dime stores, copied Woolworth's model. Ben Franklin, S. S. Kresge, and G. C. Murphy dime stores were in every American downtown and, later, in every shopping mall. With their wooden floors, glass cases, and divided open countertops filled with small items, the dime stores of the 1940s through the 1970s were a wonderland of consumer goods. Shoppers could find everything from cheap dishes to mops to hair curlers. Kids shopped for comic books and board games and even small pets like parakeets. However, dime stores usually didn't offer clothing, which people bought at specialty stores or department stores. Nor did they have tools and small appliances, which people bought at hardware stores.

Many dime stores had lunch counters, where hungry shoppers could perch on stools and order tomato soup, tuna sandwiches, and banana splits. Working people as well as shoppers often spent their lunch hour at the dime store, where they could do a bit of shopping after eating.

DEEP DISCOUNTS

In the 1960s, the five-and-dime stores began to give way to larger discount stores. One of the earliest was the Target discount store chain. Descendants of George Dayton, the original founder of Dayton's Department Store, founded the Target chain in Minneapolis in 1962. Two other big discount stores, Kmart and Wal-Mart, opened in the same year.

Like the dime stores, the discount stores offered a variety of merchandise at low prices—usually much lower than prices in department stores or individually owned stores. They were able to do this through the same policies as the dime stores, which included cash-and-carry (no credit purchases) and self-service. At stores such as Target, salesclerks are not required to know anything about the products being sold. In his book *Shoptimism*, writer and former retailer Lee Eisenberg says, "[Clerks] are trained to be a human global positioning system." He says they are trained to say, "Can I help you *find* something?—not "May I help you?"

"We go to Target sometimes. . . . We arrive and I announce that we just need one little thing. But as we walk through the doors, something happens . . . because moments later . . . I'm walking back to the car with an overflowing cart. I have no idea what just happened. And I'm pretty sure I forgot to buy the one thing I went in there for."

—Amber Dusick, *HuffPost Parents*, March 20, 2012

All the stores in a modern chain discount store are uniform. All have basically the same physical layout, with the same merchandise in the same place in each store. As in a traditional dime store, customers at discount chain stores are all treated the same way. As writer Sharon Zukin says, "The emphasis on low prices tends to minimize social class distinctions and nurtures the illusion that shopping is the same for everyone—because all of us love a bargain . . . the universal store brings rich and poor shoppers together in a uniform, one-level space."

It must be true. In 2011 First Lady Michelle Obama was spotted shopping in a Washington, DC, Target store. *ABC News* reported, "Michelle Obama proudly admitted she shopped at Target—'I'm more of a Target shopper'—and held it up as an example of how she relates to voters. She has also been known to be a fan of the discount store's clothing."

PRICING TRICKS

In the old days of the general store, prices were fluid. The shopkeeper set the price of an item. Or he might bargain with the customer or allow the customer to barter. In contrast, the early department stores set firm prices on their goods. Everybody paid the same marked price. Rowland Macy, founder of Macy's department store, introduced some smart new ideas in pricing and advertising in the 1850s. He priced everything at one to three cents below the dollar—$1.99 or $1.98, for example, instead of $2.00. This ploy, which made things seem a little cheaper, is used everywhere to this day.

To make a profit, all stores, past and present, mark their prices above what they pay for the goods they are selling. They use a variety of additional pricing strategies as well. For example, through the everyday low price (EDLP) system, a retailer promises the lowest possible prices all the time, so shoppers don't have to wait for a sale. The idea is that a store's customers will be loyal and will routinely shop there, trusting that the prices will always be low. It also saves the retailer the effort of marking down prices

Pricing items just below the nearest dollar amount has been a retail strategy for decades.

No matter where people shop, the odds are they will use a credit card to pay. Although some early stores let customers buy on store credit, it wasn't until 1951 that Frank McNamara was having a business dinner in New York City and realized he had forgotten his wallet. That embarrassing incident inspired him to come up with McNamara's Diners Club credit card. He persuaded twenty-seven New York restaurants to accept the cards as payment. Originally, two hundred cards were issued. They were cardboard instead of plastic. As time went by, the idea spread, until, by the twenty-first century, more than one billion credit cards of various kinds are in circulation in the United States.

for sales. Discount stores use this policy, which has become more popular over time. In 2012 J. C. Penney caused a stir in the retail world by announcing a move toward EDLP pricing.

Through hi-lo pricing, a retailer marks down the price of certain merchandise for a short time to draw in customers. This strategy assumes that while in the store, the customer will buy other, regular-priced items. So-called door-buster items, such as those offered on Black Friday after Thanksgiving Day, are extreme examples. Whatever profit the merchant loses on the sale item that drew the shopper into the store in the first place will be made up in that shopper's additional purchases.

CATEGORY KILLERS AND BIG-BOX STORES

Large discount stores that carry a single type of product such as office equipment or hardware are sometimes referred to as category killers. These stores include Office Depot and Staples (office and stationery supplies), Home Depot (hardware and home improvement products), and Best Buy (electronics). They offer such a large selection of products in their categories, at such low prices, that smaller individual local businesses offering similar products often can't compete.

Big-box stores, such as this Sam's Club in Arkansas, offer discounted goods in bulk. Smaller retailers find it difficult to compete with the low prices at these warehouse stores.

Retail operations such as Best Buy and Home Depot are also called big-box stores. The term refers to the huge, square buildings that often stand alone like concrete islands in a sea of parking lots. In the 1970s, when big-box stores were springing up everywhere, they were almost always located on property bought cheaply just outside town limits. People flocked to these shiny new stores, with their low prices and huge selection of goods. As a result, many small-town Main Street stores, dime stores included, died off.

In the 1980s, another kind of big-box store—the warehouse store—sprang up. Sam's Club and Costco require shoppers to pay an annual membership fee that admits them to the club. These stores are gigantic no-frills warehouse spaces. In cavernous spaces, merchandise is stacked in cartons on metal shelving divided by wide, empty aisles and lit by harsh overhead fluorescent lights. The point is not to provide an elegant shopping experience. Instead, shoppers are there to save money through buying in bulk: thirty-six-can packs of sodas; gallon jars of mayonnaise; 21-pound "locker combo" packs of beef; and giant, industrial-size containers of laundry soap. The stores also offer some individual items such as clothing and books, as well as other services that include filling prescriptions.

As in any discount store where prices seem low, customers are often lured into buying on impulse. The stores encourage this. For example, they offer samples of cookies or ravioli that taste good to hungry shoppers. The products are right there to buy, making it easy to grab a package from the refrigerator case.

> *"I'm probably the best bargain shopper ever . . . everyone needs coupons."*
>
> —Nicole "Snooki" Polizzi, reality TV personality, September 20, 2012

ON SALE!

From the beginning of consumer culture in the United States, many city department stores had bargain basements. There, unsold goods were offered at greatly reduced prices to get rid of them and make room for new inventory. The idea was pioneered by the Bargain Room at Wanamaker's Philadelphia store. One of the most famous bargain basements was Filene's Automatic Bargain Basement, opened in 1909 in Boston. Down in the poorly lit basement spaces, merchandise from sweaters to sheets was piled on big tables. Shoppers rooted through it to find the best deals.

Bargain basements offered low-priced items every day. But stores also found ways to promote sales through other kinds of promotional events. For example, fire sales were held to get rid of damaged goods. In 1859, after a gaslight accident at Macy's, store owner Rowland Macy ran a newspaper ad announcing low prices on gloves, umbrellas, men's underwear, and other goods damaged in the fire. Another idea—pioneered in 1878 by John Wanamaker

Bargain-basement shopping attracted crowds to Filene's in Boston for a sale on men's suits and topcoats in 1949. Unlike other bargain basements, Filene's had good lighting and was decorated nicely. The bargain basement sold surplus goods, factory clearance items, and overstock or closeout merchandise.

of Philadelphia—was the white sale. At that time, all bed linens were white. Wanamaker decided to put them on sale in January, when linen sales were generally slow. He sold the linens at a discount, and the white sale idea stuck. In the twenty-first century, white sales have a much broader definition. They usually involve household goods in general, and they may be held at any time of the year. And not all the items on sale are white!

A shopping day that has become almost infamous is Black Friday. On the day after Thanksgiving, many stores open very early. Some even open their doors at midnight the night before. They offer big sales to kick off the holiday shopping season. Experts disagree about the origin of the name *Black Friday*. Some contend it started in the 1960s, when traffic became so bad on sale day that police had to work a long shift. Unhappy about it, they coined the negative term. Others say that the name refers to the fact that on this busiest

Bargains still attract shoppers in large numbers in the twenty-first century. This crowd waits for Macy's in New York City to open its doors on Black Friday, the day after Thanksgiving, in 2012.

shopping day of the year, merchants make most of their profits. They are said to be "in the black" (from an accounting practice that lists profits in black ink and losses in red ink).

CHAPTER 4
MEET ME AT THE MALL

What used to be farms or woods or country crossroads have become malls. . . . If you want to find America today, this is where you have to look.

—Charles Kuralt, *CBS Reports*, "After the Dream Comes True," 1982

ntil the mid-1940s, cities were the places for the best shopping. But as U.S. soldiers came home from serving overseas in World War II, families began to migrate out of the cities and into suburbs. These new communities sprouted at the edges of cities, and as suburbs grew, the face of shopping changed too.

The outward movement from the cities came about for many reasons. One was the widespread availability of cars and the building of new highways. Americans were mobile like never before. In addition, returning servicemen and their growing families wanted affordable housing with plenty of bedrooms for their children (known as the baby boomers) and safe neighborhoods where the kids could play. Many families shunned the big cities, which they felt were too noisy, crowded, and crime-ridden. They wanted a nice house with a yard in the front and back, a garage for the car, and all the comforts of modern living. Developers responded with a building spree that soon created suburban neighborhoods across the country.

All those new homes needed washers and dryers, furniture, stoves and refrigerators, and other products galore. Laundry soap, hardware, linens, curtains, dishes,

This 1956 Maytag ad features a new washer and dryer that can launder "modern" fabrics such as rayon and acetate.

pots and pans, and lawn mowers were practical needs. All those baby boomers needed shoes and clothes and lunch boxes and shiny new bicycles. And of course, women, most of whom were stay-at-home mothers, needed to buy groceries.

During the war, American manufacturing and industry had turned most of its resources toward supplying tanks, airplanes, ammunition, uniforms, and other items for the war effort. But after the war, the nation's factories were ready and willing to supply the renewed demand for consumer goods. The squeaky-clean new suburbs did not have Main Streets as a center of the community where people shopped at local businesses. However, every suburban family had a car. The answer, it seemed, was to create new centers for shopping.

ENTER: THE STRIP MALL

As roads and highways expanded into the suburbs, supermarkets, restaurants, and other businesses grew up alongside them. Developers got the idea to group together a supermarket plus several other stores in one area. They laid out the stores in either a straight strip or an L shape, with the supermarket at one end. The stores faced the road, with a parking lot in front. Called strip malls, these car-friendly shopping destinations, with names such as Miracle Mile, sprang up everywhere.

These shopping centers, or malls, as they came to be called, continued to develop and expand. Mall designers began to change their configuration so that the stores faced away from the road and the surrounding parking lots, and toward one another. With this arrangement, developers could create spaces for people to stroll and sit within the mall. The new malls were open to the sky. As time went on, many shopping center developers added pleasant touches such as fountains and large containers of flowers. Storefronts were arranged along wide walking areas. This kind of open-air mall is still popular, especially in places such as California

Strip malls, such as this one in Queens, New York, were a new way for Americans to shop in the 1950s. Clusters of stores were grouped together with easy, outdoor parking in front.

and Hawaii, where the climate is comfortably mild year-round.

City department stores began to take notice. They realized that in the suburbs was a huge market for their kind of store. Most suburban housewives at this time didn't work outside the home. They had time and money to shop, and they were hungry for the genteel shopping experience that department stores offered. But they weren't going downtown to shop anymore, so department stores started building suburban branches.

Department stores soon became anchors for many of the new open-air shopping malls. At the beginning, one large department store sat at one end of the mall. The first such mall was Northgate Center in Seattle, Washington, which opened in 1950. Eventually, malls were anchored by not one but two department stores—one at each end. This has sometimes been called the dumbbell mall, referring to the shape of handheld weights.

"PERPETUAL SPRINGTIME"

All the early shopping centers were outdoor malls. Shoppers walked from one store to the other on sidewalks. In the 1950s, Dayton Hudson Corporation developers in Minneapolis, Minnesota, were looking to build a big new mall in the suburb of Edina. Their iconic department store, Dayton's, would be the anchor store. They wanted something new and special—a mall with two levels. Up until then, all malls were on a single level. Nobody thought shoppers would be willing to walk up to a second level. The developers also had another problem to solve—the climate. In Minnesota, winters are freezing cold, and summers are hot and humid. Shoppers at outdoor malls in that part of the county had to brave these extremes to go from store to store.

The company hired an innovative architect named Victor Gruen to design the new mall. Gruen was a visionary. He wanted to create a cleaner, neater, and suburban version of America's downtown. He wanted his new shopping mall design to provide a community center as well as a place to shop.

Gruen didn't disappoint the developers. He came up with a revolutionary idea—a fully enclosed mall. In an enclosed area, he could add a Garden Court in the central space of the mall to let in light, allow for plants and waterfalls, and to provide seating and food stalls. The mall would be built on two levels, all indoors. The upper level would be open, with low railings so the shops upstairs would be visible from below. Escalators in the center court would carry shoppers up and down, as in the interior of a department store. The new mall would be called Southdale Shopping Center.

During the three years it took to plan and build Southdale, Gruen and the builders had to come up with a new kind of heating and cooling system that would work in such a large space. The mall's year-round pleasant temperature was billed as "perpetual springtime." When the mall opened in 1956, seventy-five thousand people poured in. Southdale was a hit. Soon, people were coming

not only to shop but also to relax, snack, and socialize. The shopping center became a model for the new suburban center.

Once Southdale had led the way, malls sprang up like mushrooms all over the nation. However, not all were as attractive and innovative as Southdale, and many were cheaply built. By the 1980s, many malls were ugly blights on the American landscape. Even the executive vice president of the International Council of Shopping Centers, Albert Sussman, admitted that "some centers have abused the landscape, created eyesores, have produced chaotic traffic conditions and even disrupted local community life."

In addition to being places to shop and eat, many malls function as community centers. People can take exercise classes

MALL TALK

mall rats: people who hang out at the mall, all day, every day

mallstrosity: a giant shopping center that takes over a neighborhood

mall syndrome: the sickness or anxiety after shopping or being at the mall for too long

mall trout: any person who, when walking in the mall, travels opposite the normal flow of traffic

mall walk: walking slowly, as if you were in a mall

mall wall: a group of people walking slowly, shoulder to shoulder, in a narrow-aisled shopping plaza. The group creates a physical barricade making it impossible for others to pass on either side.

or seminars on finance at the mall. They can attend a weight-loss clinic or get a flu shot. Malls often offer entertainment in the main court, from music concerts to fashion shows to holiday events— the kinds of activities and events that used to happen downtown. In this sense, they might be thought of as the new Main Street.

BIG AND BIGGER

Once malls got to be a familiar part of the landscape, many Americans began to feel ho-hum about them. Malls offered the "same-old, same-old merchandise; same-old, same-old food selection." So mall developers added more attractions, such as multiplex movie theaters and themed restaurants, to malls. Shoppertainment was born. In addition to movie theaters, retail drama includes live music, free Wi-Fi hot spots, skating rinks, carousels, and children's play areas. These features are often the main draw, and once at the mall, people are more likely to shop as well.

It was inevitable that malls would get even bigger. The original Southdale was 800,000 square feet. It eventually expanded to 1.7

million square feet, with a multiplex movie theater and a third floor featuring shops geared toward teen shoppers. Multiple offshoot malls sprang up around it.

"You can sit in the mall and watch all the . . . people go by. . . . Everything's there—the movies and stuff, and all your friends are there."

—*The Malling of America*, quote by teenager, 1985

The granddaddy of them all is the gigantic Mall of America (MOA) in Bloomington, Minnesota (a suburb of Minneapolis). Just 6 miles from Southdale, the MOA opened its doors in 1992. It is one of the world's biggest megamalls, occupying 4.2 million square feet, all enclosed in a climate-controlled building lit by massive skylights. It boasts 520 stores, a theme park with twenty-five rides, including a roller coaster, four hundred live trees, and a 1.2-million-gallon aquarium. Shoppers choose from among fourteen movie screens and even get married in the Chapel of Love. The MOA is so big that seven Yankee Stadiums or thirty-two Boeing 747 airplanes could fit inside! The Mall of America quickly became a popular tourist destination. An attached hotel welcomes visitors by the millions from all over the United States and even from abroad.

MALL PERSONALITY

Malls have a personality designed to appeal to certain kinds of shoppers. For example, most malls cater to middle-income shoppers of all ages. They offer the same set of chain stores with predictable merchandise and familiar lighting, logos, and decor. There are no surprises. Some, such as the Town Center mall at

With 7 acres of rides and other entertainment, the indoor amusement park at the Mall of America is one of the nation's largest. Malls in the twenty-first century include hundreds of stores as well as a wide range of services and leisure activities.

Boca Raton, Florida, bill themselves as "top luxury shopping destinations." The mall decor has an upscale look, with an art installation in the central space featuring thousands of glittering golden butterflies suspended from above. In the shopping aisles, elegant flower arrangements sit atop oversize glass tables. While the mall focuses on high-end stores such as Tiffany & Co. jewelers, it also covers its bases with plenty of middle-of-the road shops, including Chico's and Skechers.

One type of mall—the kind that features factory outlet stores— appeals to just about everybody. These stores sell popular lines of housewares and designer clothing at cut-rate or modestly discounted prices. Although outlets started as places for retailers to sell excess merchandise at marked-down prices, insiders say that many designer stores now have separate lines made especially for the outlet market. Outlet shopping is hugely popular, especially at malls near tourist attractions such as Niagara Falls.

In fact, according to a spokesperson for the Niagara Falls visitors' bureau, "You'd be surprised how many bus tours come here for shopping . . . and couldn't care less about seeing the falls."

"Shop 'til you drop."

—T-shirt slogan and common saying

The Dark Side

No doubt about it, there's a side to shopping that isn't pretty. Take credit card debt. According to former retailer Lee Eisenberg, "American consumers now pack an average of four cards apiece. . . . There's irrefutable evidence that packing a card, or four or . . . more, increases . . . spending." Retailers encourage shoppers to buy on impulse instead of sticking to a shopping list and budget.

In Sophie Kinsella's 2001 novel, *Confessions of a Shopaholic,* Becky, the main character, has shopped herself deep into credit card debt. "On Monday morning I wake early, feeling rather hollow inside. I know I spent too much money on Saturday. I know I shouldn't have bought two pairs of boots . . . [and] that purple dress. In all, I spent . . . Actually, I don't want to think about how much I spent."

So-called shopaholics don't steal—they are addicted to shopping, buying boatloads of things they don't need and never use. They also rack up extraordinary debt. Some eventually seek help from twelve-step addiction programs.

Shoplifting is also part of the shopping landscape. Some people—the poor, hungry, or homeless—may steal food or clothing out of desperation. But others do it on a dare or for the thrill, even if they can afford to buy the things they steal. These compulsive shoplifters often steal because of psychological problems. According to the National Association for Shoplifting Prevention, more than $13 billion worth of merchandise is stolen each year from U.S. retailers. Between 2007 and 2012 alone, more than 10 million Americans were caught shoplifting.

Because of lower pricing, outlet malls are becoming popular worldwide. According to *Retail Traffic Magazine,* new outlets are being planned in such countries as Canada, Brazil, the United States, China, and South Korea. In 2012 there were more than 355 centers in thirty-seven countries, with an additional 83 new ones projected for 2013.

URBAN MALLS AND MARKETPLACES

Although most people think of malls along highways and in suburbs, plenty of urban malls and mall-like arrangements can be found in cities. They go by various names—arcade, marketplace, or sometimes atrium. In some city downtown areas, old or historic buildings have been converted into marketplaces with stores, restaurants, and food markets. Examples are Boston's Faneuil Hall Marketplace (the nation's first); Baltimore's Harborplace; and San Francisco's Ferry Building Marketplace, built in the city's old ferry terminal. Newly built urban malls include shopping venues such as the glittering Time Warner Center in New York City. Along with offices and upscale residences, the soaring towers house The Shops at Columbus Circle, which include more than forty shops, a huge supermarket, a fitness center, and more. In West Palm Beach, Florida, CityPlace offers shopping galore, as well as theaters, in a setting of palm trees and fountains. Centers like these provide a mall experience right in the heart of the city.

Everything old is new again. To create an atmosphere that is more appealing to twenty-first-century mall-weary shoppers, some developers are reinventing malls to resemble small-town Main Streets or old-style urban neighborhoods. They are open to the sky and feature a grid of walking streets among the stores. According to one article, they are increasingly being reinvented as "open-air 'lifestyle centers,' with condos above or offices next door."

Many existing enclosed malls have been changing their ambience in ways that encourage shoppers to linger. (Studies

Malls have come to city centers in the twenty-first century. The Shops at Columbus Circle, for example, is in the heart of Manhattan. This urban mall offers a range of specialty retail stores, restaurants, a hotel, and an upscale grocery store.

show that the longer shoppers stay in the mall, the more money they spend.) Some have created a sidewalk-café atmosphere in the center court. New designs include more comfortable seating, along with softer textures instead of metal and glass, Wi-Fi access, and flat-screen televisions for shoppers.

DEAD MALLS?

Many malls in the United States became casualties of the economic recession of 2008. Many Americans lost their jobs and their retirement savings. Businesses cut back or failed. Developers all but stopped building big new malls. When the City Creek Center in Salt Lake City, Utah, opened in 2012, it was the first new mall to open in the United States in more than six years.

During the recession, many malls that served lower- and middle-income customers failed or lost stores because shoppers were turning instead to dollar stores, thrift stores, and online retailers. In addition, many Americans are again tiring of malls. Wrote journalist Sam Walker in the *Wall Street Journal,* "There is too much sameness in retailing. If you dropped a person into most malls, they would not know what part of the country they were in."

The term *dead malls* was coined to describe shopping centers that didn't make it or are close to extinction. The website deadmalls.com lists these deserted malls and publishes shoppers' memories and histories of various shopping centers around the country.

One of the nation's most famous dead malls was the Dixie Square Mall in Harvey, Illinois, as shown in this 2010 photo. It closed in 1978 and remained largely vacant for more than thirty years until it was demolished in 2012.

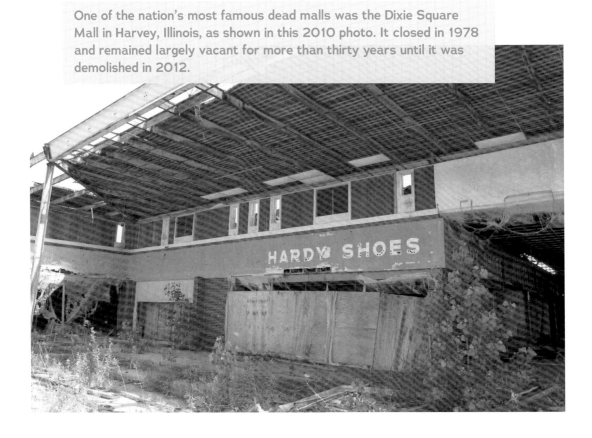

To stay afloat, some enterprising smaller malls are taking their cue from the Mall of America and welcoming new kinds of tenants to their buildings. Schools, call centers, medical clinics, and churches are renting mall space. And some malls rent out their open spaces for events such as weddings. In 2010 an executive at one mall, the Galleria in Cleveland, Ohio, even planted an indoor vegetable garden beneath its huge skylights.

Yet many malls remain prosperous. In 2012 Triple Five Worldwide, operators of the Mall of America, announced it would add a second hotel as well as more parking, more restaurants and shops—more everything.

CHAPTER 5

THE CYBER SHOPPING EXPLOSION

You might call them [online shoppers] the "new window shoppers": whenever they want something, from a flat-screen television to a 36-pack of toilet paper, they just open a new window in their Web browser.

—Megan McArdle, "The Future of Shopping," 2012

In the twenty-first century, most Americans do at least some shopping in cyberspace, spending almost $200 billion online each year. We hunt for goods on our computers, our tablets, and our smartphones. The most popular items to buy online are clothes, jewelry, and music. Booking flights and making other types of travel arrangements are another popular online sale. So are online auctions.

In fact, the first successful online shopping site was eBay, the person-to-person online auction founded by Pierre Omidyar in 1995. The original idea was for customers to bid on used items. An eBay legend says that a broken laser pointer was among the first items sold on the site. The buyer, who collected broken laser pointers, paid $14.83. Thomas Hine likens eBay to a flea market in his book *I Want That!* "Electronically rummaging through eBay is like rooting through the dusty merchandise of

E-commerce dates to the 1990s. Shoppers spend billions of dollars shopping online each year, and retailers expect electronic shopping to continue to expand quickly. The largest U.S.-based online retailers are eBay and Amazon.com.

a secondhand-seller's booth, and you keep going because the treasure may be just one layer deeper."

Internet giant Amazon had its beginnings in founder Jeff Bezos's garage. His new company shipped its first book from that location in 1995. The savvy company makes use of all kinds of technologies to sell products. Along with customer tracking, which remembers visitors to the site and makes recommendations based on previous purchases, the site also offers features such as a mobile application for smartphones and tablets. The app allows customers to shop on Amazon while on the go, getting product details and reviews, scanning bar codes for prices, and completing secure purchases. Many stores, both online and brick-and-mortar, are adopting this trend.

To get online browsers to stay on a website long enough to become buyers, retail websites add features to make the sites sticky. Free newsletters, special discounts for signing up on an e-mail list, and similar ploys attract people to a website and keep them there. Los Angeles-based FaceCake Marketing Technologies, Inc., has come up with Swivel technology, which allows online shoppers to try on clothing in a 3-D format and see themselves from all angles. The website Polyvore lets shoppers put together outfits from images of clothing on the site's database. Home furnishing sites have similar services. And of course, everyone downloads music from online music stores such as iTunes and Amazon MP3 as well as music and music videos from YouTube. In fact, downloadable music accounted for more than half of all music sales in the United States in 2012.

SHOPPING SOCIAL

After social media burst onto the scene in the early 2000s, it quickly became a natural at creating communities of fellow shoppers online. Shopping sites make it easy for friends to share their opinions about products, get and give feedback on possible purchases, and alert one another about great new stuff. Sites for brands such as GameStop or Urban Outfitters let you tell friends on Facebook that you like a new Xbox game or a cool camo skirt. You can also follow brands on Twitter and watch their videos on YouTube. One eyewear company, Warby Parker, offers Home Try On. The company will ship up to five pairs of glasses to a customer, who can try them on and post pictures via Facebook to get feedback on which pair looks best.

> ## *"I do love to shop. But I'm a social shopper. I like to do it while hanging out with my friends."*
>
> —Nicole Richie, fashion designer and actress, n.d.

Social networking helps brands build a base of loyal customers, who in turn bring in more shoppers by posting favorable comments. Sites such as Amazon play it smart by offering product reviews by customers. In her article "How Social Media Can Make Online Shopping Less Lonely," marketing executive Lauren Boyer says, "User-generated product reviews are . . . more important than ever. The Harris Interactive poll found that in the past year [2010], one-quarter of Americans increased the amount of time they spent reading product reviews online . . . [and] 60% of Americans say they value the opinions other people share on social media." Since then, those numbers have only increased.

Kaboodle, Shoplinkz, and other sites that are not product specific provide a platform for shoppers to join groups, get product suggestions, make shopping lists, and share their finds. After window shopping on the site, users click through to a retail site to buy. On Wishclouds, shoppers can discover new and recommended products from friends and even from their favorite celebrities. Shoppers can then create personalized product collections from

In the 1970s, a company called Ronco began hawking products such as the Veg-o-Matic vegetable slicer and the Pocket Fisherman fishing rod on television. The founder, Ron Popeil, enthusiastically demonstrated in two-minute ads how the products worked. Orders poured in, and a new kind of direct TV shopping was born.

Out of this trend grew infomercials. These extended commercials, usually about thirty minutes long, feature merchandise such as beauty products, dietary supplements, or cleaning products. Sometimes the ads include demonstrations. A toll-free phone number or Web address comes on-screen for ordering the product.

From these ads, it was a short step to home shopping channels. The cable television Home Shopping Network (HSN) began in 1985, when a radio manager got stuck with a big supply of electric can openers as payment from a client. Looking for a way to get rid of them, he offered them for sale. In the very next year came the QVC channel (Quality, Value, Convenience). It sold—and continues to sell—everything from exercise machines to diamonds. It's on live, 24/7. The company does an equally brisk online business and offers a smartphone app too.

multiple retailers. They can track pricing and receive price change alerts. ProductWiki gives shoppers access to product reviews and price comparisons. It also posts pros and cons and shares how many people agreed or disagreed with each pro or con.

One site, The Hunt, turns shopping into a game. Users post a photo of someone wearing a jacket or a dress they like or a cool lamp or even an app they want, along with the price they're willing to pay. Followers all over the country hunt for a match and if the person who posted the photo buys what they find, they get a gem icon posted on the website.

BRICK-AND-MORTAR FIGHTS BACK

There's no question that online retailing has hurt business for brick-and-mortar stores. Retailers are fighting back to lure—and keep—shoppers. For example, stores of all sizes offer high-tech

Surrounded by wares, Ronco founder Ron Popeil posed for this photo in 1982.

features that compete with the online experience. One clothing shop has a mirror that allows customers to put on a garment and change its color using a touch screen. In 2013 twenty branches of Bloomingdale's department store installed dressing rooms with Swivel technology, the same application some retailers use online, to allow customers to view themselves in 3-D, wearing outfits from the store. These stores also installed Swivel Virtual Stylist, which lets window shoppers on the street use touch screen technology to automatically create new looks for the window displays. Another store has a dressing room equipped with a pod that does a body scan and creates a digital 3-D model of the shopper's body. The scan helps the shopper select the garment that will fit that person's body best. Still other stores offer merchandise such as T-shirts and perfume from vending machines.

Some retailers have opted to open huge stores or to expand their existing ones. Macy's added 100,000 square feet to its

1-million-square-foot-plus store in New York's Herald Square. And in 2011, Apple Computer opened its largest store—inside New York's Grand Central Station. Part of its 23,000 square feet is devoted to social space, where commuters can browse the Web and look at Apple products while waiting for their train.

Other megastores mix shopping with entertainment on a huge scale. Jungle Jim's International Market in Ohio is a 6.5-acre grocery store that features animated, talking displays throughout the store, huge live seafood tanks, waterfalls, and more. It's so big that customers get lost. Bass Pro Outdoor World in Missouri is a sporting goods store that covers 33,000 square feet. In addition to merchandise for sale, it has a real

Shopping has expanded dramatically in American hubs of transportation. For example, the Apple store in New York's Grand Central Station is a popular place for travelers and commuters to pass time and learn about Apple's newest products.

rifle range, live crocodiles and birds, and life-size replicas of southern swamplands and forests.

Large retailers such as Macy's, Sears, and Toys R Us are getting the best of both worlds by linking their online sales to their brick-and-mortar stores. For example, when a customer makes an online purchase, an employee at the store tracks down the item and fills the order from the store. This cuts down on warehouse storage costs. In addition, many stores offer smartphone apps that let shoppers select and buy merchandise they can then pick up at the store.

POP-UPS AND OTHER HOT TRENDS

One fun retail trend is the store on wheels. Taking their cue from the popularity of food trucks, mobile shops are cruising city streets all over the country. In Hollywood, California, the pink Le Fashion Truck "boutique on wheels" posts its location for the day on Twitter and Facebook. Customers step inside to browse among racks of trendy clothes and shelves of purses, jewelry, and other accessories. As the mobile shop idea caught on, Le Fashion Truck owners Stacey Steffe and Jeanine Romo started the West Coast Mobile Retail Association. They staged the monthly shopping bazaar, The Shop Lot LA, a meet-up of trucks selling fashions and other merchandise.

Another new trend is the small, individually owned specialty shop. One type is the curated store. These shops hand-select a unique blend of merchandise in much the same way that a museum curator selects artwork for a themed exhibition. The interiors of the shops resemble quirky art galleries or antique stores. Customers are often creative people with money to spend on nonessentials—people who are tired of the cookie-cutter products at big-box and discount chain stores. A few larger stores and chains are also taking the curated approach. Examples include Anthropologie—with its uniquely styled women's clothing, accessories, and home items—and Urban Outfitters, which specializes in hip and kitschy clothes.

Another hot retail idea—the pop-up store—began back in 1999, with a Los Angeles company called Vacant. Its first stores stayed open only as long as the merchandise lasted. Other pop-ups, usually Halloween costume stores and other seasonal shops, followed. Most pop-ups last for a single day to a few months. But many become permanent if they are successful. For example, a New York store called A Startup Store Beta (later changed to Story) was originally intended to be a temporary retail boutique. But it caught on and became a permanent pop-up, changing its theme and product selection every four to eight weeks. Often online stores open brick-and-mortar pop-ups, especially during

When the Beatles' albums were reissued on vinyl in 2012, Capital Records set up a one-day pop-up shop in New York City.

the holiday shopping season. For example, in 2012, the craft marketplace site Etsy launched its first-ever pop-up store during the Christmas season in New York's SoHo neighborhood.

Large, established stores have caught on and are offering pop-ups too. Target, for example, has had a succession of pop-ups. Some have been in the stores, while others are in different venues, including one on a boat docked on New York's Hudson River.

ADVERTISING: THE BIG SELL

Pop-ups aren't just a brick-and-mortar thing. They're all over your touch screen too. Online retailers use pop-up ads to get your attention and sell more products. Any kind of advertising is basically a form of persuasion. In the early days of advertising, salesmen who traveled to country general stores and small-town stores handed out trade cards featuring pictorial advertisements for products such as Clark's O.N.T. Spool Cotton (thread) and Garden Seymour Flour. Collecting the colorful cards became a craze, and people proudly displayed their collections in scrapbooks.

Rowland Macy was a great believer in the power of advertising. From the day he opened Macy's in 1858, he regularly placed ads in the *New York Times*. These very simple ads were just a few lines of type—no images. But they pulled people in, proclaiming "Cheap Ribbon!" and "Imported Head-dresses, at one-half the cost of importation!!!"

In the 1950s, *The Hidden Persuaders,* a book by Vance Packard, shocked the American public with the then-new idea that advertising was invading the human mind in ways people weren't even aware of, manipulating them into buying things. He wrote, "Large-scale efforts [are] being made, with impressive success, to channel our unthinking habits, our purchasing decisions, and our thought processes by the use of insights gleaned from psychiatry and the social sciences. Typically these efforts take place beneath our level of awareness; so that the appeals which move us are often, in a sense, 'hidden.' . . . The sales to us of billions of dollars' worth of United States products is being significantly affected, if not revolutionized, by this approach."

Packard cited the use of motivational analysis, in which advertisers sell not just a product but also a promise. In a television ad for soda, images of people laughing and dancing at a party suggest that if we drink that soda, our life will be full of fun too. If we wash our hair with a particular shampoo or use whitening toothpaste, we, too, can be as amazingly good-looking as the girl or guy on the screen.

In the twenty-first century, advertising is everywhere. It's all over cyberspace. It's in magazines and newspapers. It interrupts television programs and flashes across computer screens on trucks and buses and buildings. On streets and highways, advertising signs and billboards—sometimes called litter on a stick or street spam—are inescapable. Author Lee Eisenberg writes that "studies show that on average each of us is exposed to between three thousand and five thousand advertising impressions a day. Most ads whip by so fast we don't register them as impressions. Think of how swiftly we browse the Internet, how link after link lands us on pages where advertising crowds the info we seek, flash-dancing across the screen."

> ## "I don't shop because I need something, I just shop for shopping's sake."
>
> —Cat Deeley, actress and host of the television show *So You Think You Can Dance*, n.d.

However, experts disagree about how influential advertising actually is. Does it really make people buy things? Or do they buy certain products for other reasons? According to Harvard Business School professor Richard S. Tedlow, the huge amount of advertising that bombards people does reinforce the idea that acquiring and owning things is desirable and even necessary, regardless of what we buy. Advertising tells us that not only is it okay to want things but that we should also go out and buy them.

WHAT'S UP NEXT?

Many observers agree that the future of shopping is largely in the hands of Gen Z, or the Net Generation, who were born into a world of computer technology, smartphones and tablets, and online networking. According to an online article by Kathy Savitt, "Generation Z-ers are tastemakers—often before they're out of elementary school. Social media has demolished all barriers to communicating about brands and products. If you can write, you can share, and Generation Z is all about sharing." Savitt points to Silly Bandz as a key example. These animal-shaped bracelets started as an online fad among nine- and ten-year olds and wound up on high-fashion runways.

Smartphone shopping apps in particular have revolutionized the shopping experience. During the holiday shopping season of 2012, industry watchers noted a sharp rise in the use of smartphones and tablets to find deals, compare prices, share shopping information, and buy. A lot of smartphone buying takes place online. But brick-and-mortar retailers are also getting into the act with their own apps for in-store use that send out real-time sale alerts and coupons, allow customers to scan bar codes, and make checkout easier. Retailers including Target, Home Depot, and Saks Fifth Avenue offer in-store Wi-Fi. At the same time, retailers are doing everything they can to prevent showrooming, the practice of identifying a product in the store, then using a smartphone to order the same thing for less money from a competitor online.

It all adds up to more choices for consumers. In the near future, the line between in-store and online shopping will continue to blur, as more and more stores offer online ordering with in-store pickup as well as smartphone checkout and other features. Some retailers are also letting shoppers upload video clips of themselves to the retailer's site, modeling jeans or showing off a camera they just bought. Stores such as Sports Authority and Old Navy are partnering with Shopkick and other sites to offer reward points and other perks. And as international e-commerce explodes, shoppers are finding they can order just about anything from just about anywhere in the world—without leaving their own backyard.

GLOBAL MARKETPLACE

E-commerce makes shopping a truly international experience. Many companies around the world offer online information about products in more than one language to make international purchasing easier. Traffic to U.S. retail sites from international visitors is high, and many U.S. companies offer overseas shipping. Working out payments and shipping overseas can be complicated, but retailers believe that solving these problems is well worth the effort. Writes Julia Wilkinson on the website EcommerceBytes .com, "Even though not everyone in the world looks to buy from the United States, and international shipping can be a headache, one thing is clear: there are international buyers out there who want stuff from the U.S. . . . sellers who don't offer it may be missing out on sales."

Although the United States is the world's biggest online market, other countries, especially China, Brazil, and Russia, are rapidly expanding their online traffic. According to corporate consultant A. T. Kearney, in 2012 China had 513 million Internet users (the largest online population in the world) and 164 million online shoppers. China's largest domestic online shopping site is Taobao. For Chinese users, *"Taobao-ing"* has become a lifestyle. They can buy a huge variety of products from Taobao shops and communicate with buyers and sellers, as well as watch movies in Taobao Cinema, make travel arrangements, share news and chat with friends, charge their phones, and play video games. Soon, through sites that make communication in other languages easier, U.S. shoppers will be able to shop on Taobao and similar sites.

One thing is certain: whether we stroll through a mall, log on to our tablets, or browse via smartphone, the urge to shop—and the fun and thrills that many people get from shopping—isn't going away anytime soon.

SOURCE NOTES

4 Larry Freeman, *The Country Store* (Watkins Glen, NY: Century House, 1955), 8.

10 Jack Larkin, *The Reshaping of Everyday Life, 1790–1840*. (New York: Harper & Row, 1988), 208–209.

10 Don Marquis, "My Memories of the Old-Fashioned Drummer," *American Magazine* 107 (February 1929): 152–154.

16 Ann Satterthwaite, *Going Shopping: Consumer Choices and Community Consequences* (New Haven, CT: Yale University Press, 2001), 25.

16 Maude Hart Lovelace, *Betsy and Tacy Go Downtown* (New York: Thomas Y. Crowell Company, 1943), 123–125.

18 Moses King, *King's Handbook of New York City*, 1892, quoted in *The Drive to Protect the Ladies' Mile District*, n.d., http://www.preserve2.org/ladiesmile (October 10, 2012).

19 Theodore Dreiser, *Sister Carrie* (1900; reprint, Philadelphia: University of Pennsylvania Press, 1998), 324.

20 King, *King's Handbook of New York City*, 1892.

21 Satterthwaite, *Going Shopping*, 42–43.

21 Wendt, Lloyd, and Herman Kogan, *Give the Lady What She Wants! The Story of Marshall Field and Company* (Chicago: Rand McNally, 1952).

22 Nancy F. Koehn, "An Essay from 19th Century U.S. Newspapers Database: Consumerism and Consumption," Graduate School of Business Administration, Harvard University, Gale Cengage Learning, n.d., http://www.gale.cengage.com/pdf/whitepapers/gdc/Consumerism_whtppr.pdf (November 9, 2012).

24 Laura Byrne Paquet, *The Urge to Splurge: A Social History of Shopping* (Toronto: ECW Press, 2003), 114.

26 Satterthwaite, *Going Shopping*, 128.

28 Dreiser, *Sister Carrie*, 22.

29–30 Karal Ann Marling, *Merry Christmas! Celebrating America's Greatest Holiday* (Cambridge, MA: Harvard University Press, 2000), 91.

30 William R. Leach, *Land of Desire: Merchants, Power, and the Rise of a New American Culture* (New York: Vintage Books, 1993), 65.

32–33 Jan Whitaker, *Service and Style: How the American Department Store Fashioned the Middle Class* (New York: St. Martin's Press, 2006), 10.

33 Roxanne Roberts, "Once There Was a Woodies," *Washington Post*, June 23, 1995, quoted in Satterthwaite, *Going Shopping*, 128.

34 Ron Rosenbaum, "Barbara Kruger's Artwork Speaks Truth to Power," *Smithsonian*, July–August 2012, http://www.smithsonianmag.com/arts -culture/Barbara-Krugers-Artwork-Speaks-Truth-to-Power-160281585 .html?c=y&page=1 (April 16, 2013).

35 Frances Trollope, *Domestic Manners of the Americans* (New York: Alfred A. Knopf, 1949), 401–402.

37 Ilene Beckerman, *Love, Loss, and What I Wore* (New York: Algonquin Books of Chapel Hill, 1995), 76.

38 Lee Eisenberg, *Shoptimism: Why the American Consumer Will Keep on Buying No Matter What* (New York: Free Press, 2009), 20.

39 Amber Dusick, "Shopping at Target," *HuffPost Parents*, March 20, 2012, http://www.huffingtonpost.com/amber-dusick/shopping-at -target_b_1351414.html (October 3, 2012).

39 Sharon Zukin, *Point of Purchase: How Shopping Changed American Culture* (New York: Routledge, 2004), 69.

39 Mary Bruce, "Spotted: Michele Obama Shopping at Target," September 29, 2011, *ABC News*, http://abcnews.go.com/blogs/politics/2011/09/spotted -michelle-obama-shopping-at-target/ (November 8, 2011).

43 Nicole Polizzi, Twitter feed @snooki, September 20, 2012, https://twitter .com/snooki (March 8, 2013).

46 William Severini Kowinski, *The Malling of America: An Inside Look at the Great Consumer Paradise* (New York: William Morrow, 1985), 47.

51 Ibid., 122.

52 Eisenberg, *Shoptimism*, 29.

53 Kowinski, *The Malling of America*, 36.

55 Edwin McDowell, "America's Hot Tourist Spot: The Outlet Mall," *New York Times*, May 26, 1997, http://www.nytimes.com/1996/05/26/us/america-s-hot -tourist-spot-the-outlet-mall.html?pagewanted=2&src=pm (March 8, 2013).

55 Eisenberg, *Shoptimism*, 251–252.

55 Sophie Kinsella, *Confessions of a Shopaholic* (New York: Dial Press, 2001), 137.

56 Emily Badger, "The Shopping Mall Turns 60 (and Prepares to Retire)," *Atlantic Cities*, July 13, 2012, http://www.theatlanticcities.com/arts-and -lifestyle/2012/07/shopping-mall-turns-60-and-prepares-retire/2568/ (March 6, 2013).

58 Sam Walker, "Hair Salons, Hot Tubs and . . . Oh, Yeah, Basketball," *Wall Street Journal*, March 27, 1998, W6.

60 Megan McArdle, "The Future of Shopping," *Daily Beast*, December 2, 2012, http://www.thedailybeast.com/newsweek/2012/12/02/megan-mcardle-on -how-luxury-will-win-the-shopping-wars.html (March 11, 2013).

61–62 Thomas Hine, *I Want That! How We All Became Shoppers* (New York: HarperCollins, 2002), 106.

63 Nicole Ritchie, "Shop Quotes," *Brainy Quote.com*, n.d., http://www .brainyquote.com/quotes/keywords/shop.html#Rs23fjAbIDM8RcRt.99 (March 8, 2013).

63 Lauren Boyer, "How Social Media Can Make Online Shopping Less Lonely," *Mashable.com*, November 10, 2010, http://mashable.com /2010/11/18/social-shopping-loneliness (March 12, 2013).

69 Robert M. Grippo, *Macy's: The Store. The Star. The Story* (Garden City, NY: Square One, 2009), 25.

69–70 Vance Packard, *The Hidden Persuaders* (1957; reprint, New York: Ig Publishing, 1980), 31.

70 Eisenberg, *Shoptimism*,108.

70 Cat Deeley, "Shop Quotes," *Brainy Quote.com*, n.d., http://www .brainyquote.com/quotes/keywords/shop.html#Rs23fjAbIDM8RcRt.99 (March 8, 2013).

71 Kathy Savitt, "3 Ways Companies Can Reach Generation Z," *Mashable. com*, April 8, 2011, http://mashable.com/2011/04/08/marketing-generation-z (November 14, 2012).

72 Julia Wilkinson, "Sell More Internationally: What Foreign Buyers Want," April 1, 2012, *EcommerceBytes.com*, http://www.ecommercebytes.com/cab /abu/y212/m04/abu0308/s03 (March 14, 2013).

SELECTED BIBLIOGRAPHY

Badger, Emily. "The Shopping Mall Turns 60 (and Prepares to Retire)." *Atlantic Cities*, July 13, 2012. http://www .theatlanticcities.com/arts-and-lifestyle/2012/07/shopping -mall-turns-60-and-prepares-retire/2568 (March 6, 2013).

Dreiser, Theodore. *Sister Carrie*. 1900. Reprint, Philadelphia: University of Pennsylvania Press, 1998.

Eisenberg, Lee. *Shoptimism: Why the American Consumer Will Keep on Buying No Matter What*. New York: Free Press, 2009.

Farrell, James J. *One Nation Under Goods: Malls and the Seductions of Shopping*. Washington, DC: Smithsonian Books, 2003.

Freeman, Larry. *The Country Store*. Watkins Glen, NY: Century House, 1955.

Grippo, Robert M. *Macy's: The Store. The Star. The Story*. Garden City Park, NY: Square One, 2009.

Hine, Thomas. *I Want That! How We All Became Shoppers*. New York: HarperCollins, 2002.

Housewright, Tipton. "Ten Retail Trends for 2012—and Beyond." *Shopping Center Business*. July 2012. http://www .shoppingcenterbusiness.com/index.php?option=com _content&view=article&id=553:ten-retail-rends-for-2012 -and-beyond-shopping-center-business&catid=26:tenant -spotlight&Itemid=453 (October 18, 2012).

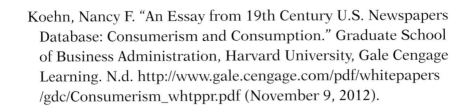

Koehn, Nancy F. "An Essay from 19th Century U.S. Newspapers Database: Consumerism and Consumption." Graduate School of Business Administration, Harvard University, Gale Cengage Learning. N.d. http://www.gale.cengage.com/pdf/whitepapers /gdc/Consumerism_whtppr.pdf (November 9, 2012).

Kowinski, William Severini. *The Malling of America: An Inside Look at the Great Consumer Paradise*. New York: William Morrow, 1985.

Larkin, Jack. *The Reshaping of Everyday Life, 1790–1840*. New York: Harper & Row, 1988.

Leach, William R. *Land of Desire: Merchants, Power, and the Rise of a New American Culture*. New York: Vintage Books, 1993.

Matthews, Christopher. "Reports of the Shopping Mall's Death Have Been Greatly Exaggerated." *Business Time*. August 10, 2012. http://business.time.com/2012/08/10/reports-of-the -shopping-malls-death-have-been-greatly-exaggerated /#ixzz2CiCMdJHW (December 4, 2012).

Packard, Vance. *The Hidden Persuaders*. 1957. Reprint, New York: Ig Publishing, 1980.

Paquet, Laura Byrne. *The Urge to Splurge: A Social History of Shopping*. Toronto: ECW Press, 2003.

Ritzer, George. *Enchanting a Disenchanted World: Continuity and Change in the Cathedrals of Consumption*. Los Angeles: Pine Forge. 2010.

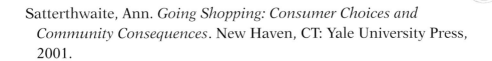

Satterthwaite, Ann. *Going Shopping: Consumer Choices and Community Consequences*. New Haven, CT: Yale University Press, 2001.

Spears, Timothy B. *100 Years on the Road: The Traveling Salesman in American Culture*. New Haven, CT: Yale University Press, 1995.

Sutherland, Anne, and Beth Thompson. *Kidfluence: The Marketer's Guide to Understanding and Researching Generation Y—Kids, Tweens, and Teens*. New York: McGraw-Hill, 2003.

Tedlow, Richard S. *New and Improved: The Story of Mass Marketing in America*. New York: Basic Books, 1990.

Turow, Joseph, and Matthew P. McAllister, eds. *The Advertising and Consumer Culture Reader*. New York: Routledge, 2009.

Whitaker, Jan. *Service and Style: How the American Department Store Fashioned the Middle Class*. New York: St. Martin's Press, 2006.

Yarrow, Kit, and Jayne O'Donnell. *Gen Buy: How Tweens, Teens, and Twenty-Somethings Are Revolutionizing Retail*. San Francisco: Jossey-Bass, 2009.

Zollo, Peter. *Wise Up to Teens: Insights into Marketing and Advertising to Teenagers*. Ithaca, NY: New Strategist, 1999.

Zukin, Sharon. *Point of Purchase: How Shopping Changed American Culture*. New York: Routledge, 2004.

BOOKS

Behnke, Alison, Cynthia Overbeck Bix, Kate Havelin, and Katherine Krohn. Dressing a Nation. Minneapolis: Twenty-First Century Books, 2012.
This series covers American fashions through many historical time periods. Each volume shows the trends and influences on clothing designs, hairstyles, and accessories for women, men, and children at all levels of society.

Cherry, Robin. *Catalog: The Illustrated History of Mail Order Shopping*. New York: Princeton Architectural Press, 2008.
This entertaining book offers a visual history of American catalogs.

Kelly, Caitlin. *Malled: My Unintentional Career in Retail*. New York: Penguin, 2011.
Kelly offers a fascinating firsthand account of one woman's experience in working at a retail clothing store.

Klaffke, Pamela. *Spree: A Cultural History of Shopping*. Vancouver, BC: Arsenal Pulp, 2003.
This book offers an entertaining survey of shopping in modern America. It includes sidebars about a variety of high-interest subjects, such as celebrity shoplifters, garage sales, and more.

Levine, Judith. *Not Buying It: My Year Without Shopping*. New York: Free Press, 2007.
The author chronicles her yearlong experiment with cutting back on shopping.

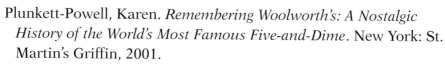

Plunkett-Powell, Karen. *Remembering Woolworth's: A Nostalgic History of the World's Most Famous Five-and-Dime*. New York: St. Martin's Griffin, 2001.
Plenty of vintage photos and interesting text tell the story of America's greatest five-and-dime stores.

Quart, Alissa. *Branded: The Buying and Selling of Teenagers*. Cambridge, MA: Basic Books, 2003.
This study shines a light on the sometimes shocking reality of how corporations market their products to teenagers, as well as on teens who participate in ways that include working for corporations in exchange for products.

Scheff, Anna. *Shopping Smarts: How to Choose Wisely, Find Bargains, Spot Swindles, and More*. Minneapolis: Twenty-First Century Books, 2012.
This book explores shopping from all angles and shares advice on how teens can "shop smart." Supplemented with articles and information from *USA Today*, it delivers firsthand stories of real teens facing shopping situations.

Whitaker, Jan. *The World of Department Stores*. New York: Vendome Press, 2011.
Generously illustrated with photos and illustrations, this book provides a look at department stores of the world.

WEBSITES

Deadmalls
http://www.deadmalls.com
This website lists malls that have closed up and "died" or are half-empty. It also features shoppers' memories and histories of various shopping centers around the country.

Mall of America
http://www.mallofamerica.com
This is the official site of the Mall of America, currently the nation's largest megamall.

Sears Archives
http://www.searsarchives.com
The company chronicles the history of its catalog as well as its retail stores on this website.

TrendWatching
http://www.trendwatching.com
This website tracks consumer trends around the world, providing fascinating information about trends, insights, and innovations.

Radio

These four excerpts from National Public Radio chronicle various aspects of shopping, old and new:

Henn, Steve. "Do These Pants Make Me Look . . . ? Body Scans for a Better Fit." *All Things Considered*. NPR audio, 5:10. June 4, 2012. http://www.npr.org/blogs/alltechconsidered/2012 /06/04/154284798/do-these-pants-make-me-look-body-scans -for-a-better-fit.

———. "To Keep Customers, Brick-and-Mortar Stores Look to Smartphones." *All Things Considered*. NPR audio, 4:25. March 27, 2012. http://www.npr.org/blogs/alltechconsidered/2012/03/27 /149463201/to-keep-customers-brick-and-mortar-stores-look -to-smartphones.

Kaufman, Wendy. "Forget the Register: Stores Use Mobile to Make Sales on the Spot." *All Things Considered*. NPR audio, 4:37. December 10, 2012. http://www.npr.org/blogs /alltechconsidered/2012/12/10/166890714/forget-the-register -stores-use-mobile-to-make-sales-on-the-spot.

Whitaker, Jan. "Big Stores Changed Retail with Hands on Shopping." Interview by Audie Cornish. *All Things Considered*. NPR audio, 4:51. December 11, 2012. http://www.npr.org /2012/12/11/167000621/big-stores-changed-retail-with-hands -on-shopping.

VIDEOS

NBC. "America's Oldest General Store Closes," *NBC Nightly News* video, 0:27. July 29, 2012. http://video.msnbc.msn.com/nightly -news/48387264#48387264.
This sweet and sentimental tribute shows the closing of Gray's General Store, one of the oldest continuously operating country stores in the nation.

"History and Science of Shopping: Burt Wolf Travels & Traditions." YouTube video, 2:20. July 30, 2009. http://www.youtube.com/ watch?v=6peAhAD2hKM.
Narrator Burt Wolf hosts a quick shopping trip in New York City, from streetside flea markets to designer boutiques.

LERNER

SOURCE

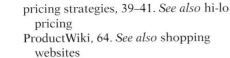

PHOTO ACKNOWLEDGMENTS

The images in this book are used with the permission of: Illustrations © Emily Harris/Independent Picture Service; © Amana Productions Inc./ Getty Images, p. 5; AP Photo/Stephan Savoia, p. 6; © MPI/Stringer/ Archive Photos/Getty Images, p. 7; © Bettmann/CORBIS, pp. 8, 11, 22; Library of Congress pp. 9 (LC-USZ62-50934), 21 (LC-USZ62-74723), 23 (LC-USZ62-43074); © Old Paper Studios/Alamy, p. 13; The Granger Collection, New York, pp. 14, 25, 29; © Dorling Kindersley/Getty Images, p. 15; © Independent Picture Service, p. 16; Mid-Manhattan Library/ Picture Collection, Miriam and Ira D. Wallach Division of Art, Prints and Photographs, The New York Public Library, Astor, Lenox and Tilden Foundations, p. 19; Chicago Historical Society, DN-0007502, Chicago Daily News, Inc., p. 26; Emmet Collection, Miriam and Ira D. Wallach Division of Art, Prints and Photographs, The New York Public Library, Astor, Lenox and Tilden Foundations, p. 27; National Museum of American History, Kenneth E. Behring Center/Smithsonian Institution, neg. 316700, p. 31; © The New York Public Library/Art Resource, NY, p. 36; © The Museum of the City of New York/Art Resource, NY, p. 37; AP Photo/Don Heupel, p. 40; Sarah Conrad/Reuters/Newscom, p. 42; © George Silk/Time Life Pictures/Getty Images, p. 44; © Stan Honda/AFP/ Getty Images, p. 45; © Apic/Hulton Archive/Getty Images, p. 47; © William Gottlieb/CORBIS, p. 49; Norton and Peel, Minnesota Historical Society, p. 51; © TIMO GANS/AFP/Getty Images, p. 54; © Brent Winebrenner/Loenly Planet Images/Getty Images, p. 57; © Michael Tercha/Chicago Tribune/MCT via Getty Images, p. 58; © Pixellover RM 7/ Alamy, p. 61; AP Photo/Reed Saxon, p. 65; © Rudy Sulgan/CORBIS, p. 66; © Emmanuel Dunand/AFP/Getty Images, p. 68.

Front cover: © Fuse/Getty Images (bag); © Emily Harris/Independent Picture Service (background).

Main text set in New Aster LT Std 11/15.
Typeface provided by Adobe Systems.

ABOUT THE AUTHOR

Cynthia Bix grew up in Baltimore, Maryland. Family visits to historical sites throughout the United States sparked her early interest in American history, crafts, and everyday life.

Now living in the San Francisco Bay Area, Cynthia loves to write about anything and everything. In her more than thirty nonfiction books for children and adults, she has written about such diverse subjects as the fine arts, natural science, and domestic arts. She has also written how-to-do-it books about all kinds of activities, from making impressions of animal footprints to planting a garden. One of her most recent titles for young readers is *Petticoats and Frock Coats: Revolution and Victorian-Age Fashions from the 1770s to the 1860s*. In addition to writing, she edits books for both children and adults.